MW00989567

Essential Question
How do traditions connect people?

Grandfather's Basket

by Lee DeCora Francis
Penobscot/HoChunk
illustrated by Anna Vojtech

Chapter 1
Muhmum's Words

It was early morning on a summer day in 1960. *Doonk! Doonk! Doonk!* Rodney's eyes slowly opened as a small grin appeared on his face. He lay listening to the familiar sound that signaled it was time to begin his day. Sliding gently out of bed, he quietly grabbed his clothes, looked at his sleeping brothers, and tiptoed to the stairs. He splashed cool water on his face and brushed his teeth before heading out into the yard. His grandfather, Muhmum, was already hard at work. His grandmother, Nokomis, was busy scrubbing laundry on the washboard but stopped to give Rodney his hug as she did every morning.

Long strips of ash tied in bundles were piled near the entrance to the shed. Freshly cut ash trees waited along the riverbank for their turn. It was a beautiful sight and almost made Rodney forget his worries. He reached the area where he worked with Muhmum and sat on one of the logs that lined the shed.

Doonk! Doonk! Doonk! Rodney watched his grandfather raise the blunt side of the axe again, pounding the mark he made on the log. Muhmum glanced up. The intensity of Rodney's gaze told him that something was wrong. He put down his axe and rested on the log next to his grandson.

Muhmum knew Rodney was worried about leaving the reservation for school in the fall. It would be the first time he attended a school that wasn't full of his own people. Muhmum placed his hand on Rodney's shoulder and smiled. He reminded his grandson that he wouldn't be going far. The school was in the neighboring town just across the river. He'd be able to come home every afternoon.

They sat for a few moments more and soon Rodney held the axe in his hands. He took his spot next to the log and pounded it with the back of the axe like his grandfather taught him. With each swing, he thought about his Muhmum's words. When his grandfather was a boy, he had to go to a school far from home and wasn't able to return until he was older. At the school, he wasn't allowed to speak his language or play with his relatives. Rodney knew his school would be different but he still wished he could stay home and make baskets.

Chapter 2
Baskets

Most boys Rodney's age helped prepare the ash to make baskets. While Rodney continued to pound the ash, he remembered how difficult it was when he first started. But it was an important job, one he needed to learn how to do for his people. Everyone worked together, young and old, to survive. Many supported their families with the art and knowledge of making baskets. Some families focused on making larger, sturdier baskets that people used for more difficult work. Others focused on the smaller, fancier baskets that tourists liked to collect.

Rodney's family made all types of baskets. Both of his parents helped make baskets in the evenings after working in the factory sewing shoes. His grandmother often gathered with other women. They would work on their baskets all day. Each woman had her own particular style. Rodney's grandmother liked adding curls to her work, while her friend made points with the small strips of ash. Another woman added color to her baskets.

Rodney's grandfather made bigger baskets, as did many other men on the island. He made laundry baskets, potato baskets of all sizes, and pack baskets. His pack baskets were the best, and Rodney wanted to make packs just like his.

All week, Rodney helped his grandfather pound and split ash. There would be plenty for the baskets. More and more tourists took the ferry across the river now to buy baskets at the Penobscot Indian Basket Shop. Rodney's family had worked carefully making sure there were plenty of baskets. They placed some at the basket shop, and they sent many to the coast for other family members to sell.

Rodney wondered about the people that bought those baskets. He thought about all the places their baskets might travel. He knew that his family needed to make more for the fall, and he worried about how his grandfather would keep up once he started school.

Rodney admired the way his grandfather Muhmum moved through his workshop. Paths had been worn into the floor. Every item had its place. His little brothers were not allowed into the workshop most of the time. Rodney was thankful for this because he found them irritating.

As a young boy, Rodney loved to sit on a stool and watch the baskets take form. He was fascinated at the way the strips went together. As Rodney grew older, Muhmum asked for his assistance, showing him how to construct the baskets.

Today, the two worked side by side. They placed basket bottoms onto wooden blocks that would help give them the right shape. Muhmum teased his grandson by reminding him of their most recent trip to gather ash. Rodney smiled as his grandfather retold the story.

They had one log left to carry to the shore. Rodney bent down, reached under the tree, and hoisted it onto his shoulder. He felt something move along his neck and down his chest. He looked at the ground and screamed at the sight of a brown snake. He retreated from the woods as quickly as possible. There wasn't much that scared Rodney, but snakes definitely did. He despised them.

Chapter 3
New Shoes

The next day was spent weaving the baskets that sat waiting in the corner. Rodney loved weaving—he was especially skilled at it. Often, other men from the family would lend a hand. It was during these times that Rodney learned about his relatives through the stories they shared.

Many had left the reservation as young men. They had lied about their age to join the Army because they wanted to protect their homelands. His cousins, Claude and LeRoy, were both sixteen when they left for Korea. He listened closely and pictured the stories in his mind. Rodney realized that each basket held the history of his people.

Rodney didn't have a big pack basket of his own yet. He wondered when he would finally wear one with pride.

When Rodney was a little boy, his grandfather would carry him on his back in a pack basket. Once he asked his grandfather if he would fall through. Muhmum replied, "Packs are strong like the endurance of our ancestors. It will hold you."

Rodney's favorite of his grandfather's packs was the one he rode in as a young boy. It had been painted a light blue many years ago. Some of the color had faded, but it was still Rodney's favorite.

The Saturday before school, Rodney came downstairs and greeted Nokomis. Two slices of toast waited for him at the table next to a cup of tea. Nokomis ate breakfast and talked about her plans for the day. She asked Rodney to go into town with her.

The Landing was busy that morning. People waited for the ferry with goods in hand. Canoes lined both shores.

At the store, Nokomis held a crisp, white shirt to Rodney's chest. Next, they found a proper pair of pants to fit his long legs. His grandmother then selected a pair of shiny leather shoes. Rodney knew she'd have to forfeit something she needed in order to buy the shoes. Rodney suggested a different pair, but his grandmother insisted on the shoes she held in her arms. She needed her grandson to look handsome at his new school. On the way home, Rodney wondered how he might pay her back.

Sunday night, Rodney tried not to think about starting school the next day. *Tomorrow will be fine,* he thought. He'd been in town many times before. Last year, he went with his grandmother when his people were finally allowed the right to vote. He knew the town's people, and that was what bothered him. Some people there treated him differently because he was Penobscot. *You can do this. You can do this. You will do this,* he told himself as he settled into bed.

Rodney looked at himself one more time before leaving. He strolled down the road toward the ferry. At the dock, he found his cousin waiting for her first day of school to begin too. They talked and laughed as they waited for the ferryman to arrive. Soon, he felt a familiar hand on his shoulder. He turned to see Muhmum smiling at him. Muhmum took off his pack and handed it to his grandson.

His grandfather adjusted the straps, saying, "This is your pack now. I've had this pack for many years. It's traveled with me to many places. No matter where I went, it connected me to home. That's what it'll do for you too." Rodney hugged his grandfather and thanked him. The he climbed into the boat. Rodney wore the pack with honor. He felt the strength from his grandfather's basket against his back. He looked across the water to see his grandfather still standing on the shore watching him. Rodney waved goodbye before starting up the hill toward the school.

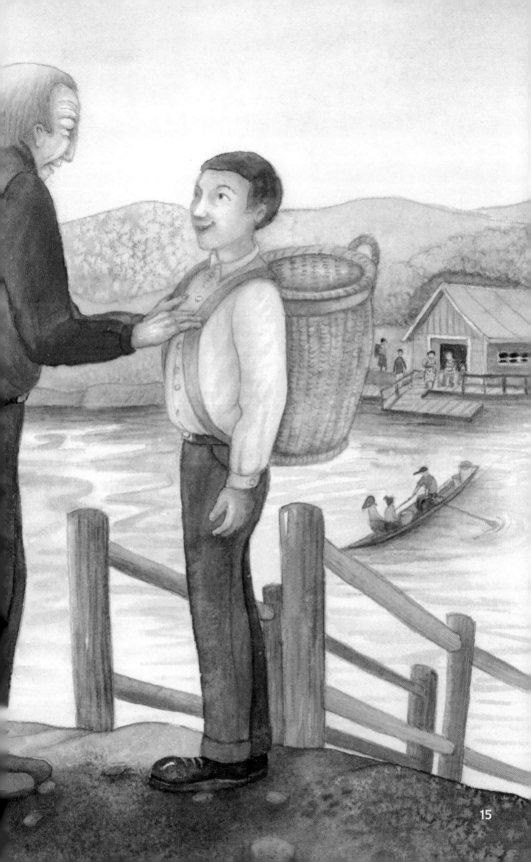

Summarize

Use the most important details from *Grandfather's Basket* to summarize the story. Your graphic organizer may help you.

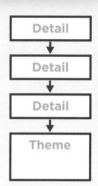

Text Evidence

1. How is this story an example of historical fiction? GENRE

2. Why is learning to make baskets important to Rodney? THEME

3. On page 9, what is the denotation of *fascinated*? What is the connotation? CONNOTATION AND DENOTATION

4. What gives Rodney the confidence to face his first day of school? WRITE ABOUT READING

Compare Texts
Read about the Penobscot Nation.

Penobscot Nation

The Penobscot people, or penewahbskew, come from what is now called Maine. Their main reservation is located in the Penobscot River watershed called Indian Island. Historically, the territory of the people included land and waterways in Maine and part of Massachusetts. The Penobscot are part of the Wabanaki Confederacy along with the Passamaquoddy, Micmac, and Maliseet people. The Wabanaki have inhabited this land for at least the past 10,000 years.

According to the latest U.S. Census in 2010, about 600 Penobscot people live on Indian Island.

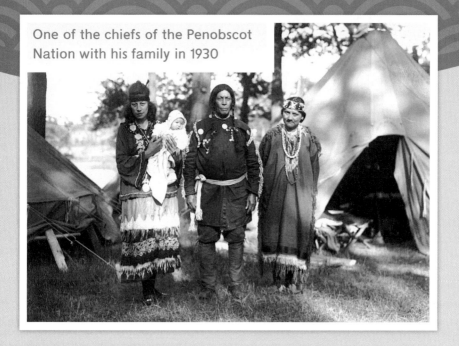
One of the chiefs of the Penobscot Nation with his family in 1930

The Penobscot people, along with other Wabanaki, had a deep knowledge of the waterways and land. They built and lived in sophisticated villages. They traveled freely throughout their homelands using their understanding of resources and seasonal changes. Today, the Penobscot still have that knowledge, but a much smaller land base. The people still carry on the traditions of their ancestors.

The Penobscot Nation also has a very old, independent government. Tribal leadership consists of a chief, vice chief, tribal council, and a tribal representative. The Nation has many important programs and departments such as education, healthcare, natural resources, and elder and youth services.

Every aspect of the Penobscot culture was and still is connected to the Penobscot River. The river is extremely important to the tribe. The Penobscot Nation focuses a lot of attention on protecting this body of water and its tributaries. There are many islands located within the river itself that are part of the tribe's reservation lands. The health of the water directly affects the health of the people and their culture. The Penobscot River is easily their most precious resource.

The Penobscot River provides food, water, and many other resources for the Penobscot.

Make Connections

Why is the Penobscot River important to the Penobscot Nation? ESSENTIAL QUESTION

What is a Penobscot tradition that Rodney learned from his grandfather? TEXT TO TEXT

Focus on Genre

Historical Fiction Historical fiction tells a story that is set in the past. It often gives information about a real event and can show real people who were living at the time. Historical fiction gives the reader an understanding of life in the past.

Read and Find *Grandfather's Basket* takes place in the past and includes realistic characters, events, and settings. The characters in the story are made up, but the story is inspired by the Penobscot Nation's tradition of making baskets.

Your Turn

Native Americans have a tradition of oral storytelling. The stories teach about the past. Choose a person or an event in your family that you could tell a story about. You can make up some details to add interest, but base your story on facts. Practice telling your story until it sounds and feels right and then share it with others in your group or class.